PRIVATE EYE

Colemanballs
9

A selection of quotes,
most of which originally appeared
in PRIVATE EYE's
'Colemanballs' column.

Our thanks once again to all the readers
who sent us their contributions,
and to whom this book is dedicated.

COLEMANBALLS TOP TEN

PLACE	NAME	ENTRIES
1	DAVID COLEMAN	116
2	MURRAY WALKER	83
3	SIMON BATES	52
4	TED LOWE	38
5	JOHN MOTSON	27
6	BRIAN MOORE	24
7	HARRY CARPENTER	22
8	RON ATKINSON	21
9	KEVIN KEEGAN	18
10	BOBBY ROBSON	16

COMPOSITE TOTAL FIGURES COMPILED BY THE NEASDEN INSTITUTE OF STATISTICS, E&OE

PRIVATE EYE

Colemanballs
9

Compiled and edited by
BARRY FANTONI

Illustrated by Larry

PRIVATE EYE

Published in Great Britain
by Private Eye Productions Ltd,
6 Carlisle Street, London W1V 5RG,
in association with Corgi Books

©1998 Pressdram Ltd
ISBN 1 901784 11 8
Designed by Bridget Tisdall
Printed in Great Britain by
Cox and Wyman Ltd, Reading

Athletics

"It's become a fascinating duel between three men."

DAVID COLEMAN

"Here is Michael Johnson, the world champion, whose world record is not held by him but by Butch Reynolds."

DAVID COLEMAN

"There's Nascimento, the pacemaker from Brazil, running a sensible race, and sharing out the work with his compatriot from Argentina..."

BRENDAN FOSTER

"It must be an amazing feeling to win the Marathon over that distance."

CLAIRE BALDREY

"That would be a marvellous way for Linford Christie to bow out in his last International debut."

COMMENTATOR, RADIO 5 LIVE

"Five qualify of right — the first five."

DAVID COLEMAN

"This runner is 87 years old — he'll remember this day for a long time!"

DAVID COLEMAN

"...and that bronze medal is worth its weight in gold."

DAVID COLEMAN

"A massive sigh of relief there from Bubka, no show of emotion at all."

STUART STOREY

"Morcelli has the four fastest 1500-metre times ever. And all those times are at 1500 metres."

DAVID COLEMAN

"And the headwind was 3.1 against her..."

DAVID COLEMAN

"Colin Jackson, reflecting on what's to come…"

DAVID COLEMAN

"The 5,000 or so volunteers are breaking their backs to make sure it's a success."

RADIO 4 (on the Paralympics)

"But the main group just a few yards behind the main group…"

BRENDAN FOSTER

"The critical thing in hurdling is not to make mistakes."

DAVID COLEMAN

"Nineteen Kenyans started in that race — and they finished 1-2-3."

DAVID COLEMAN

Boat Race

"Winning is everything, but only the losers know how that feels."

BOAT RACE COMMENTATOR, BBC1

Classic FM

"Disappointing news for Beethoven as his 9th Symphony drops 9 places in our Hall of Fame…"

JAMIE CRICK

"So it's Mexico, Mexico, Mexico. Speaking of Mexico, here's a piece from Brazil."

HENRY KELLY

"A further 450 Connex trains were grounded today."

CLASSIC FM NEWS

"…and talking of the devil, at number 18 it's Agnus Dei…"

NICK BAILEY

Cricket

"To win a three match series, you really want to be looking at winning two of the matches."

MIKE ATHERTON

"It's now two-nil to England with two to play — and they're both to come."

MARK NICHOLAS

"Oh, and here comes Caddick to bowl again from the pavilion end again… well, I don't suppose he'll mind if I read the scores between his balls."

HENRY BLOFELD

"The breeze is getting up and we can just about see Umpire Shepherd's trousers filling up with wind."

JONATHAN AGNEW

"When you restrict a side to 170, 99 times out of 10 you feel confident."

MICHAEL ATHERTON

"We didn't have metaphors in our day. We didn't beat about the bush."

FRED TRUEMAN

"With the retirement of Dickie Bird something sad will have gone out of English cricket."

JOHN MAJOR

"I'm glad two sides of the cherry have been put forward."

GEOFFREY BOYCOTT

"He's standing on one leg like a horse in a dressage competition."

HENRY BLOFELD

"If England lose, they'll be the losers."

BOB WILLIS

"History is there to be made but it doesn't happen very often."

GEOFFREY BOYCOTT

"We might be in for more rain than maybe we're going to get."

HENRY BLOFELD

Cycling

"The trouble is, all year I haven't had the ability to go faster than possible."

CHRIS BOARDMAN

Football

"Okay, so we lost, but good things can come from it — negative and positive..."

GLENN HODDLE

"What the difference is between three minutes to three and five o'clock, I'm not sure."

LINCOLN CITY FC CHAIRMAN

"Last week in Russia we saw the name 'McCoist' spelt in the Acrylic alphabet. Quite a sight…"

ALISTAIR ALEXANDER

"His brain was going as quick as his legs and he was in two minds."

ALAN BRAZIL

"…Tony Adams — he's the rock that the team has grown from."

RON ATKINSON

"30 minutes to go, and it's still 1-0 a-piece."

COMMENTATOR, SCOT-FM

"I've had this sneaking feeling throughout the game that it's there to be won…"

RON ATKINSON

"Liverpool are playing quite well, even now they've got the ball."

HOWARD WILKINSON

"…and still we have a game on our hands. As long as it remains that way, then that's the way it will be."

RON JONES

"We are not as bad a team as people give us credit for!"

MARK BARHAM

"It's a tale of two systems, John, and both exactly the same."

MARK LAWRENSON

"Goalkeepers — they're not born today until they're in their late twenties or early thirties…"

KEVIN KEEGAN

"He [Ben Thatcher] is only 20, but he's already played for the England Under-21 side."

"KICK OFF LIVE"

"It's like the Alamo for Dunfermline. They're waiting for General Custer to appear."

DEREK JOHNSTONE

"There's a snap about Liverpool that just isn't there!"

RON ATKINSON

"They'll perhaps finish in the top three. I can't see them going any higher."

DON HOWE

"Unfortunately, we don't get a second chance. We've already played them twice."

TREVOR BROOKING

"Italians everywhere, and here's Petrescu — a Romanian."

ALAN GREEN

"…and there's the Swiss manager with the manicured moustache."

BRIAN MOORE

"She [the England team's faith healer] gives the players a shoulder to talk to."

NEIL WEBB

"Pearce with the kick… the last throw for England."

BRIAN MOORE

"And the FA thinks it's really unfair that UEFA have thrown all their apples behind Germany."

ADAM MINOT

"The game has gone rather scrappy as both sides realise they could win this match or lose it."

KEVIN KEEGAN

"Defensively, if there's a weakness in this Brazilian side, it's at the back."

TONY LOCKWOOD

"He has those telescopic legs that can turn a Leeds ball into an Arsenal one."

JOHN MOTSON

"We signed to play until the day we died, and we did."

JIMMY GREAVES

"Stoichkov is pointing at the bench with his eyes."

DAVID PLEAT

"Lombardo speaks much better English than what people realise."

MARK GOLDMAN (Crystal Palace FC owner)

"One or two people are streaming away."

COMMENTATOR, RADIO 5 LIVE

"The crowd are off their feet…"

JONATHAN LEGARD

"This game's about winning and losing — and if you win, that means you've beaten someone."

GRAHAM TAYLOR

"...they've done the old-fashioned things well; they've kicked the ball, they've headed it..."

RON ATKINSON

"You can't do better than go away from home and get a draw..."

KEVIN KEEGAN

"That youngster is playing well beyond his 19 years... that's because he's 21."

DAVID BEGG

"Everything he [David Mellor] is involved in, he goes in hard and he goes in deep."

SAM HAMMAN (Wimbledon FC owner)

"Leeds United are enjoying more of the possession now that they have the ball."

SIMON BROTHERTON

"The ageless Dennis Wise — now in his thirties…"

MARTIN TYLER

"There's Bergkamp standing on the halfway line, with his hands on his hips, flayling his arms about."

JOHN SCALES

"There are two schools of thought on the way the rest of this half is going to develop; everybody's got their own opinion…"

KEVIN KEEGAN .

"The tide is very much in our court now."

KEVIN KEEGAN

"Scholes hits the goalpost — he could hardly have hit that any better."

BBC WORLD SERVICE

"The gelling period has just started to knit."

RAY WILKINS

"If anyone scored against Milan it had to be a goal."

RAY WILKINS

"This could be a repeat of the final."

KEVIN KEEGAN

"Feyenoord were on very thin water there."

COMMENTATOR, EUROSPORT

"They're not doing as well in the league as they've done."

ROY HODGSON

"We were a little bit outnumbered there — it was two against two."

FRANK McCLINTOCK

"Talk us through the match from your bird's eye view on the pitch…"

HELEN CHAMBERLAIN

"And with his magnetic hands he secures the ball."

ALAN GREEN

"He is putting his mouth where his hopes are!"

SKY

"We have more non-English players in our league than any other country in the world."

GORDON TAYLOR

"…I've lost count of the times I've played in that fixture. Each one was a memorable occasion…"

TREVOR STEVEN

"It was the most humiliating feeling you could ever wish for."

B GOULD

"David Seaman is not great when he's got to kick the ball. With his feet…"

ALAN HANSEN

"That's a wise substitution by Terry Venables: three fresh men, three fresh legs."

JIMMY HILL

"In a sense it's a one-man show… except there are two men involved, Hartson and Berkovic, and a third man, the goalkeeper."

JOHN MOTSON

"He's been a constant threat in Chelsea's thorn."

COMMENTATOR, CHANNEL 5

"That's a question. When did a country have three losing nations in European competitions?"

RON ATKINSON

"If anyone can put a cog in the Germans' wheel, it's Glenn Hoddle."

RAY WILKINS

"It was a definite penalty but Wright made a right swan-song of it."

JACK CHARLTON

"Good luck to Arsenal against Borussia Münchengladbach tonight — now there's a team you wouldn't want to play at Scrabble."

PAT SHARPE

"The World Cup is every four years, so it's going to be a perennial problem."

GARY LINEKER

"Blackburn Rovers have a bottomless pit of money and now they've sold Alan Shearer for 15 million pounds, that pit is even deeper."

COLIN GIBSON

"I do not want to put labels around his [Joe Cole's] head and nooses around his neck that he cannot live up to."

TONY CARR, (West Ham Youth Team Manager)

"The match will be shown on Match of the Day this evening. If you don't want to know the result, look away now as we show you Tony Adams lifting up the cup for Arsenal."

STEVE RIDER

"It's going to be a particularly hairy game from now on... now they've got that goal under their tails."

JOE ROYLE

"He [Arsene Wenger] gives us unbelievable belief."

IAN WRIGHT

"Liverpool will be without Kvarme tonight, he's illegible."

JIMMY ARMFIELD

"And he's treading on dangerous water there…"

RON ATKINSON

"Poor Miklosko. Hasn't had to make a save yet he's let three goals in."

TREVOR FRANCIS

"Ferguson hasn't scored since the opening day of the season… he's not a natural striker."
(5 mins later) "Ferguson. At last a goal from him… natural instincts from a former Scottish striker."

ROB PALMERS

"I played against Sammy Lee — he was the same age as me at the time."

JOHN ALDRIDGE

"You weigh up the pros and cons and try to put them in chronological order."

DAVE BASSETT

"Di Matteo's taken to playing in midfield like a duck out of water."

PETER OSGOOD

"I think in international football you have to be able to handle the ball."

GLENN HODDLE

"The problem is that there's no middle ground in football any more — and we are in that middle ground."

JOE ROYLE

"Di Matteo has just blown his nose on the touchline."

SIMON BROTHERTON

"We need the players, because without the players we wouldn't have a team."

HOWARD WILKINSON

"The FA are still optimistic about England's bid to stage the World Cup in twenty thousand and six."

PETER SNOW

"Lama came out to get the cross with his white gloves trailing in front of him."

JOHN MURRAY

"Yes, they've come out with all cylinders flying, Peter."

LUTHER BLISSETT

"It could be bad news for Andy Sinton. His knee is locked up in the dressing room."

GEORGE GAVIN

"And Blackburn have made an immediate start to this game."

JOHN MOTSON

"Kevin Keegan has now tasted the other side of the fence…"

DAVE MERRINGTON

"What an opening for Shutt…"

JOHN HELM

"If England get a point, it will be a point gained as opposed to two points lost."

MARK LAWRENSON

France '98

"Tony Banks described the English fans arrested in Marseilles as 'Brain dead louts'. This goes for me as well."

SECRETARY, FOOTBALL SUPPORTERS ASSOC

"He's holding his right arm and signalling with his left."

JOHN MOTSON

"Croatia don't play very well without the ball."

BARRY VENISON

"Football's always easier when you've got the ball."

KEVIN KEEGAN

"You feel if Chile could just organise, they could hammer Austria nil-nil."

JON CHAMPION

"And you don't score 118 goals in 120 games by missing from there."

KEVIN KEEGAN

"You wonder if the sands of time are catching up with them."

KEVIN KEEGAN

"England bowed out of the World Cup with their heads held high last night..."

BRUCE MILLINGTON

"And Seaman, just like a falling oak, manages to change direction."

JOHN MOTSON

"All the Paraguayan players sank to their feet..."

DAVID PLEAT

"It was still moving when it hit the back of the net."

KEVIN KEEGAN

"...he's made endless runs into that position."

RON ATKINSON

"The good news for Paraguay is that they've gone two-nil down so early on."

KEVIN KEEGAN

"That's the 34th time he's played for his country here tonight."

BRIAN MOORE

"...of course it's great to see Paul Gascoigne starting at the other team's goal and run the whole length of the field to score."

HARRIET HARMAN

"They [the Belgian team] were just standing around looking at each other, and that's no remedy for success."

CHRIS WADDLE

"He's pulling off defenders' shoulders and making it difficult for them!"

KEVIN KEEGAN

Golf

"I think I can just see the corner of the ball."

JACK NEWTON

"…defeated but victorious."

COMMENTATOR, SKY TV

"Bernhard Langer is considered a good putter from this range, irrespective of his reputation."

PETER ALLIS

"…and you could see Parnevik's heart visibly drop…"

PETER ALLIS

Horses

"Further Flight seems to get better and better, although he's not as good as he was."

DEREK THOMPSON

"Dickey inside her going well…"

STUART STOREY

"Pilsudski is out in front, but only by virtue of the fact that that's where he is."

COMMENTATOR, RADIO 5

Literally

"He's literally holding his head in his hands within himself."

PETER DRURY

"There is literally no time for the players to breathe in this game."

JOE LYDON

"Rangers have been so far ahead. Now they've gone on to, literally, another planet."

GEOFF WEBSTER, BBC RADIO SCOTLAND

"My grandfather, King George VI, who had literally been catapulted onto the throne..."

PRINCE EDWARD

"And here's Pat [Eddery], picking the horse up literally."

DEREK THOMPSON

"Mike Pigg there literally eating up the ground."

HUGH PORTER

"You could literally hear the silence 50 miles away."

SIMON BATES

"…the majority of kids these days are literally physically illiterate."

DUNCAN GOODHEW

"And the England team are, literally, dissolving in the centre circle."

RADIO 5 LIVE

"And as Mansell comes into the pits, he's quite literally sweating his eyeballs out."

ITV

Mediaballs

"Just before we go — Diana. It spells 'an aid' backwards. Something to think about on this sad morning."

FIONA PHILLIPS

"And let's not forget the other people in this tragedy — such as Dodi, whose death seems to have taken a back seat this week."

ANNA FORD

"The Queen Mother, 97 years old on 4th August. A day she hoped she would never see…"

SKY NEWS

"The Queen's speech today is unprecedented, but just how unprecedented is it?"

HOWARD HUGHES

Motor Sport

"Schumacher is the fastest man on the track. He's going round quicker than anybody else."

MURRAY WALKER

"…and Edson Arantes di Nascimento, commonly known to us as Pele, hands the award to Damon Hill, commonly known to us as, er… Damon Hill…"

MURRAY WALKER

"Can you imagine the amount of money the first successful woman in Formula One will make? She'd have endorsements coming out of every orifice!"

JOHN INVERDALE

"At last a smile from Jacques Villeneuve to match his bleached hair…"

JONATHAN LEDGARD

"He's not going to produce a winner but if he produces second it'll be the next best thing."

MURRAY WALKER

"We've had drivers going off left, right and centre..."

MURRAY WALKER

"The conditions at the Nurburgring are much better than last year's Grand Prix of Europe, when the weather conditions were indescribably bad: driving rain, heavy mist and bitter cold."

MURRAY WALKER

"Well, 'if' is a big word in Formula One — 'if' is Formula One spelt backwards…"

MURRAY WALKER

"And Nakano tries to avoid being passed by his teammate Trulli, which should in fact be quite easy, because Trulli is going more slowly than his teammate Nakano."

MURRAY WALKER

"There are only four cars on the circuit at the present moment and two of them are in the garage."

MURRAY WALKER

"Except for his car, he's the only man on the track…"

MURRAY WALKER

"There are lots of 'if's in motor racing and 'if' is a very long word."

MURRAY WALKER

"He [Nigel Mansell] is a highly experienced driver with an unblemished record of accidents."

SAMANTHA COHEN

Music

"Chiltern FM: the station with more music and now even less talk. And, coming up in a minute, all the latest gossip from Katy."

DJ, CHILTERN FM

"John Lennon would have had his 56th birthday today. How old would he be if he was still alive?"

PAULA WHITE

"My life is so full of surprises, nothing surprises me any more."

KIM WILDE

"Beethoven, Kurtag, Charles Ives, Debussy – four very different names."

PRESENTER, RADIO 3

"You could hear everyone's eyebrows going higher and higher into their foreheads…"

MEMBER OF 'PIECE BY PIECE'

Oddballs

"I do have dreams and nightmares, but when I wake up I instantly forget them and wipe the sheet clean."

MICHAEL BILLINGTON

"Is it the way he left or the manner of his leaving?"

ANNA FORD

"There are thousands of people out there who haven't claimed for deafness because they haven't heard about it."

RETIRED MAJOR

"That was in the '70s and '80s, but now we're in the '90s and nearly the '20s."

TONY GREEN

"I have a claustrophobia for heights."

LADY ELIZABETH "KANGA" DALE

"Once you've had a bull terrier, you'd never want any other dog. I've got two bull terriers, a rottweiler and a bulldog."

JULIAN DICKS

"Before we had central heating, we used to put our socks and pants on the radiator to warm them up."

"DR" NEIL FOX

"Punch is a humorous magazine."

JERRY HAYES

"It could have been divine intervention or just an act of God…"

NEWSREADER

"Gay men have changed their sexual behaviour, but it's extremely difficult to keep it up year after year."

JAMIE TAYLOR

"...and he would stand there staring at him with his eyes..."

COMMENTATOR, BBC

"I have no history of violence — I can knock down every point she has made."

GEOFFREY BOYCOTT

"I've got ten pairs of trainers. That's one for every day of the week."

SAMANTHA FOX

"A practising Roman Catholic, he [Sonny Bono] is survived by his fourth wife Mary and four children from his various marriages."

THE TIMES

"It was the straw that just completely tore her apart…"

FRIEND OF NAOMI CAMPBELL

"And later we'll go over to Rome, where three paintings have been stolen by Van Gogh and Cezanne..."

JAMES PROCTOR

"The women of Turkey are furious. Armies of 'Natashias', prostitutes from Georgia, are invading Turkey to cream the men."

OLENKA FRENKIEL

"If you've ever suffered from insomnia, you'll know what a nightmare it can be."

CARON KEATING

"Britain was very different in my grandfather's day. There were children walking around without proper feet."

3RD EARL ATLEE

"It's difficult to underestimate the warmth and affection here for Mother Theresa."

IAN WILLIAMS

"Walking down the street, I saw — to be perfectly precise — ten, twenty, fifty, one hundred beggars…"

TOMMY BOYD

"It's nice to see so many umbrellas here in spite of the rain."

RICHARD KEYES

"After all, we've had two thousand years' notice of the Millennium…"

JOHN HUMPHRYS

"Locals object to the public being allowed into Princess Diana's grave."

NEWSDIRECT RADIO

"Ten years ago, only a third of schoolchildren went on to higher education. Now it is 33 per cent."

TEACHERS' SPOKESMAN

"Ffyona Campbell, you always seemed to me a very determined person: someone who was really driven…"

JUDY FINNIGAN

"The man's body was found on 22 June, 1996, although pathologists believe he may have died six months before his death from gunshot wounds."

NEWSREADER

"Up here, winter can strike at any time of the year."

TRAILER FOR 'WILDERNESS WALKS'

"It's like learning to play golf. Just when you think you've cracked it, they move the goalposts."

ADRIAN LOVE

"It has been the German Army's largest peacetime operation since World War 2."

ITN

"Welcome to our morning soiree."

DANNY BAKER

"Mars must be one of the most inhospitable places on earth."

BBC RADIO LEEDS PRESENTER

"He is a harmless vagrant who already has a criminal record for rape…"

JOHN SUCHET

"The Met Office says there will be some dark spells tonight."

NEWSREADER

"…and I see that in the centre of the square there is a large conical erection with a virgin on it."

DILLY BARLOW

"...every time he does it my heart leaps into his mouth for him."

JOHN BARRATT

"Heathrow could be a lot less congested if there were not so many people milling around."

SIR MICHAEL BISHOP

"I am right at the bottom of the lake where Byron wrote much of his best-loved poetry."

BOB WALKER

"Four sheep for every Welshman."

HEADLINE, INDEPENDENT ON SUNDAY

"Here were four boys plucked from obscurity
like cuckoos from their nest."

JONATHAN ROSS

"Israeli troops have this morning entered the
Arab township of Hebron, in search of the
perpetrators of the recent suicide bomb attacks
in Jerusalem, whom they believe are in hiding
there."

CNN NEWS INTERNATIONAL

"I don't want to cut anybody else's nose off to spite our face."

ABCTV AUSTRALIA

"Abattoirs don't make a killing…"

ABATTOIR DIRECTOR MR DUGGINS

"She's (Myra Hindley's) spent longer in jail than she's been alive."

PETER DEELEY

"We're the ones with our necks on the table."

EUROTUNNEL DIRECTOR

"As soon as the cashflow stops, they start to crumble like a pack of cards…"

KEN RUNDLE

"You seem to be a man who likes to keep his feet on the ground — you sail a lot."

ALAN TITCHMARSH

"You would like to go to the place of your birth; a place you've never been."

NICKY HORNE

"We've had to beg, steal and borrow computers."

CHIEF CONSTABLE, NOTTS CONSTABULARY

"You can almost taste the cedar-wood from the oak barrels."

OZ CLARKE

"Gay sex at 16 is to be law."

COMMENTATOR

"...you've been playing with fire and now you're reaping the whirlwind."

DR IAN BANKS

"The silence is getting louder."

DAVE WOODS

"Eurotunnel have poured cold water on their own researchers."

NEWSREADER

"Most cars on our roads have only one occupant — usually the driver."

CAROL MALIA

"The allegations were denied as the police continue to question the alligators."

REPORTER, NBC

Politics

"It [MPs' pay rise] is a red hot political football!"

REPORTER, ITN

"I'm talking about measures that should have been taken in the slaughterhouses, and we know that there have been some black sheep there…"

GAVIN STRANG

"If is a very big preposition."

JOHN MAJOR

"He [President Clinton] should lay it on the table and let the American people decide."

PETE KAYE (US Congressman)

"I don't make predictions. I never have and I never will."

TONY BLAIR

"They [the Scottish Tories] have a blank sheet of paper, brim full of ideas."

KENNY MACINTYRE

"After the ceasefire in Ireland tourism went shooting up."

JIM WALLACE MP

"A Cabinet Minister's son has been arrested for selling drugs… The Prime Minister is being kept up to speed with developments."

NEWSCASTER, RADIO ULSTER

"The Loyalists say they won't just lie down and walk away."

DENNIS MURRAY

"Due to the economic situation in that country, the Government was forced to put fighting of the forest fires onto the back burner."

BBC INDONESIAN CORRESPONDENT

"The single most important two things we can do…"

TONY BLAIR

"…the State of the Union Address… empowered him further, to show him as a man on the job."

DR JOHN WATSON

"That's just the tip of an ice-cube."

NEIL HAMILTON

"This is not a time for soundbites, but I feel the hand of history on my shoulders."

TONY BLAIR

"We start today in Belfast where the big guns are being wheeled out for the campaign for a yes vote in the referendum on the peace deal."

SYBIL RUSCOE

"Let's talk about Hillary Roddam Clinton, who'll be going on American breakfast TV in a few hours' time. Of course, she's pulled it off for her husband in the past…"

PRESENTER, BBC NEWS-24

"We must look at them with a piece of salt!"

GORDON BROWN

"Sir Nicholas Scott will tonight make a final attempt to stand at his Kensington and Chelsea constituency."

RADIO 4 NEWS

Question & Answer

MICHAEL BARRYMORE: And what do you do for a living?
CONTESTANT: I'm a gravedigger.
MB: And do you have any hobbies?
CONTESTANT: Yes, I have an allotment.

ITV

ED STEWART: You were 58 two days ago.
CONTESTANT: That's right.
ED STEWART: Can I ask how old you were?
CONTESTANT: 58.

RADIO 2

LISTENER: My most embarrassing moment was when my artificial leg fell off at the altar on my wedding day.
SIMON FANSHAWE: How awful! Do you still have an artificial leg?

TALK RADIO

RADIO COMMENTATOR NO.1: You're having problems reading the time there, aren't you?
RADIO COMMENTATOR NO.2: It's these new digital clocks, I can't get the hang of them. I much prefer a good old hand job...

HOKONUI GOLD, NEW ZEALAND

SHANE RITCHIE: What's your name?
CONTESTANT: Eva.
SHANE RITCHIE: Short for?
CONTESTANT: Eva.

ITV

CALLER: There are too many foreign players in the league.
MARK LAWRENSON: Why do you think that is?
CALLER: Because there are a lot of them.

RADIO 5

IAIN ANDERSON: And what's a lassie from Turiff doing with an Arsenal scarf round her neck, then?
LASSIE FROM TURIFF: I'm an Arsenal supporter.

BBC RADIO SCOTLAND

JOHN DUNN: So where have you been today?
CONTESTANT: Hull Docks.
JOHN DUNN: Where's that?
CONTESTANT: Hull.

BBC RADIO 2

DAVID VINE: He's playing like a world champion.
JOHN VIRGO: Well, he is a world champion.

BBC2

FRIENDS ACTOR: I was eating in a restaurant and a fan handed me his baby.
GABY ROSLIN: A live baby?

CHANNEL 4

TONY LEWIS: So, it's the 40th anniversary of Test Match Special. How long has it been going?
CHRISTOPHER MARTIN-JENKINS: Forty years...

RADIO 4

PHILIP CHAPMAN: So, what can we expect in this mime performance?
ARTIST: Well, it's a visual show...

RADIO NOTTINGHAM

KILROY-SILK: Did you mean to get pregnant?
GIRL: No. It was a cock-up.

ITV

PRESENTER: So, you haven't won the TV then, but what would you have done with it?
MEMBER OF AUDIENCE: Er… watched it.

CHANNEL 5

QUESTION: Who is the current editor of Private Eye?
CONTESTANT: Bernard Ingham.

CHANNEL 4

CALLER: I arrived in Birmingham in April 1956.
PAUL ROSS: What time of the year was this?

TALK RADIO

SUSANNAH SIMONS: So what does 'artist in residence' mean?
STEPHEN ISSELIS: I think it means you're an artist and you're resident somewhere.

CLASSIC FM

INTERVIEWER: You're hauling a very big sledge.
EXPLORER: Yes, about 200lbs.
INTERVIEWER: So how much stuff do you have to take with you?
EXPLORER: About 200lbs.

RADIO 4

SHOEMAKER: Sometimes we use French leather.
JOHN ELEY: Where do you get that from?
SHOEMAKER: France!

BBC RADIO SUFFOLK

BRADLEY WALSH: And your other daughter's called?
CONTESTANT: Scarlet.
WALSH: Why's that?
CONTESTANT: She's named after the Llanelli rugby team.
WALSH: And they play in?
CONTESTANT: Llanelli.

ITV

ED DOOLAN: What does a Venus Fly Trap catch?
CALLER: Flies.

BBC RADIO

PROFESSOR ANTHONY CLARE: You were an only child. Do you know why?
URI GELLER: My parents didn't have any other children.

RADIO 4

RICHARD MADELEY: I understand you have a little lad of 12.
CALLER: Yes, that's right.
MADELEY: Is he a boy or a girl?
CALLER: A boy.

CARLTON

MIKE ALLEN: How is your Latin?
CONTESTANT: Comme ci, comme ça.
MIKE ALLEN: Good.

TALK RADIO

OZ CLARKE: So, you've won the British Avant-Garde Hairdresser of the Year Award — what does that mean?
HAIRDRESSER: Well it means I'm the British Avant-Garde Hairdresser of the Year.

BBC1

DUTCH COMMENTATOR: What's your first impression of the PSV stadium?
KENNY DALGLISH: I've been here before.
DUTCH COMMENTATOR: What's your second impression of the PSV stadium?
KENNY DALGLISH: It's very nice.

NEDERLANDS 2 TV

TIM LOVEJOY: What football team do you
support?
CALLER: Woking.
TIM LOVEJOY: Where do they play?
CALLER: Woking.

SKY SPORTS

PRESENTER: What has been the reaction to
this new ban?
SMITHFIELD SPOKESPERSON: It hasn't
caused a problem at all. As soon as our traders
opened for business this morning, the customers
bought all the oxtail we had. They went mad...

GLR AT SMITHFIELD MEAT MARKET

CALLER: What was wonderful was my ten-year-old son scoring a goal for his football team.
TOMMY BOYD: How old is he?
CALLER: Ten years old.

BBC

PRESENTER: Your new book is called 'Glenn Hoddle: The Man and the Manager' — now what's it all about?
GUEST: Glenn Hoddle.

'UNDER THE MOON'

INTERVIEWER: This afternoon you're going to be judging the Face of '96 competition. What will you be looking for?
MODEL: Well, you've got to be 5ft 8in.

BBC1

MRS BRADSHAW: These are vegetarian pasties.
LADY THATCHER: Lovely — and have you put much meat in them?

BBC2

INTERVIEWER: What was the last book or books you read?
HOWARD KENDALL: My own autobiography which, interestingly enough, was written by the Guardian's Ian Ross.

GUARDIAN

RICHARD KEYES: So Roy, do you think that to win this championship you'll have to finish above Manchester United?
ROY EVANS: Actually Richard, we'll have to finish above everyone.

SKY SPORTS

RICHARD ORFORD: Where are you calling from?
CALLER: Southampton.
ORFORD: Southampton! Just down the road from here in Cowes on the Isle of Wight…

THE BIGGER BREAKFAST

JOHN CHAMPION: Well, we've just had the comical sight of the fourth official inflating a *third* ball with a bicycle pump… I've always said UEFA officials have an inflated opinion of themselves, David.
DAVID PLEAT: There are seven trees to every person in this city…

RADIO 5 LIVE

PETER MANDELSON: We've just invested £2.3 billion in schools.
CALLER: What's that in real terms?
MANDELSON: In real terms, it's £2.3 billion.

RADIO 5 LIVE

PHIL COLLINS: Bags have been left, bags have been lost, the Tour Manager didn't get his wake-up call…
INTERVIEW: I understand someone didn't wake up this morning.
PHIL COLLINS: Yeah… the Tour Manager.
INTERVIEWER: What happened?
PHIL COLLINS: He didn't get his wake-up call.

BBC1

DJ: So what subjects are you studying then?
YOUNG CALLER: ... I.T., History, Art.
DJ: Art?! So you're aiming to be the next Stravinsky?

ATLANTIC 252

INTERVIEWER: How would Diana like to be remembered?
DR DAVID HOPE: I think she would like to be remembered for the ordinary — er — but extraordinary person which she was.

RADIO 4

PAUL REYNOLDS: What did he [Prince Philip] say to you?
PERSON IN CROWD: He asked me where I was from.
PAUL REYNOLDS: And where are you from?
PERSON IN CROWD: Malaysia.
PAUL REYNOLDS: So what did you say to him?
PERSON IN CROWD: I said "I am from Malaysia."

RADIO 5 LIVE

PETER SISSONS: Which issue do you think was closest to Diana's heart?
JENNY BOND: It was with the landmines issue that she really found her feet.

BBC NEWS

DERMOT MURNAGHAN: When did you hear of the death?
PENNY JUNOR: 5am — when you phoned me.

ITN

CHRIS TARRANT: How old is she?
CALLER: Three and a half.
CHRIS TARRANT: Is it the terrible twos then?

CAPITAL RADIO

Rugby

"Look at the black shirts, swarming like bumble bees, keeping their fingers in the dyke without any trouble at all."

BILL MCLAREN

"As Phil De Glanville said, each game is unique — and this one is no different to any other."

JOHN SLEIGHTHOLME

"We were, in rugby terms, dyslexic."

JACK ROWELL

"We don't want to see hookers going down on players."

STUART BARNES

"Every Rugby international is totally unique — and this one is just the same."

ENGLAND PLAYER

Snooker

"If Ronnie O'Sullivan's going to win this match, he's going to have to win it himself."

CLIVE EVERTON

"And this is where precision needs to be precise."

JOHN SPENCER

"If you don't play them, the balls will never forgive you."

JOHN VIRGO

"This is reminiscent of any session of snooker that you've seen or that you are likely to see."

JOHN PULMAN

"Ronnie O'Sullivan, twenty years of age, but his shoulders are much older…"

TED LOWE

"Look at Stephen Hendry sitting there. Just staring into space — totally focused."

DAVID VINE

"He put all his eggs in one basket and pulled out a cracker."

DENNIS TAYLOR

Tennis

"Rusedski finally looking like the player he has looked like throughout these championships."

CHRIS BOWERS

"After she came back, she was hitting the ball like a pistol."

VIRGINIA WADE

"Washington, haring to the net like a terrier…"

TONY ADAMSON

"I'm actually partisan on either side."

VIRGINIA WADE

"Novotna's holding her nerve — her nerve, of course, has always been her Achille's Heel."

JOHN BARRATT

Unicycle Hockey

"Unicycle hockey could be just the sport for you, but you'll have to get your skates on if you want to take part..."

SPORTS PRESENTER, CHANNEL 5